Ist National Distinguished Lecture on Sociology of Sanitation

SANITATION IN INDIA WITH FOCUS ON TOILETS AND DISPOSAL OF HUMAN EXCRETA

Ist National Distinguished Lecture on Sociology of Sanitation

SANITATION IN INDIA WITH FOCUS ON TOILETS AND DISPOSAL OF HUMAN EXCRETA

by

Professor Leela Visaria

Eminent Sociologist and Former Director,
Gujarat Institute of Development Research, Ahmedabad

Under

Sulabh International Centre for Action Sociology
in Collaboration with
Sulabh International Social Service Organisation
in
National Distinguished Lecture Series on
Sociology of Sanitation

GYAN

ISBN: 978-81-212-1277-9

Price: ₹ 90

First Published, 2015

Published by

Gyan Publishing House
23, Main Ansari Road
Daryaganj, New Delhi-110002
Phones: 23282060, 23261060
Fax : 91-11-23285914
E-mail: books@gyanbooks.com

Laser Typesetting: Future Computer, Delhi

Printed at: G. Print Process, Delhi

Cataloging in Publication Data—DK
Courtesy: D.K. Agencies (P) Ltd. <docinfo@dkagencies.com>

Visaria, Leela, author.
1st national distinguished lecture on sociology of sanitation / by Professor Leela Visaria.
pages cm
Includes bibliographical references.
ISBN 9788121212779

1. Sanitation—Social aspects—India. 2. Sanitation—Government policy—India. I. Title. II. Title: First national distinguished lecture on sociology of sanitation.

DDC 363.720954 23

Preface

The National Conference on Sociology of Sanitation held on January 28-29, 2013, in New Delhi, was culmination of four decades of working in the area of sanitation, and vindication of which was the mass participation by sociologists from all over India to show their unanimous and unstinted support to my concept of "Sociology of Sanitation" to be included as a part of sociology. It was affirmation by sociologists and social scientists to study sanitation as a sociological subject.

In order to continue the dialogue on the Sociology of Sanitation, I decided to hold National Distinguished Lecture series to be delivered by a leading sociologist for bringing impetus to the enrichment of corpus of knowledge on sociology of sanitation. I was indeed honoured and privileged, when Professor LeelaVisariaji, Eminent Sociologist and Former Director, Gujarat Institute of Development Research, Ahmedabad, Gujarat accepted to deliver the First National Distinguished Lecture, on January 10, 2014.

The distinguished lecture is being printed for mass dissemination to strengthen the domain of sociology of sanitation among sociologists, social scientists, professionals, experts and policy makers and for all who are actively engaged in the field of sanitation.

Dr Bindeshwar Pathak
Sociologist and Social Reformer

Leela Visaria
Honorary Professor
Ph.D. (Sociology)
visaria@gidr.ac.in, lvisaria@gmail.com

Leela Visaria **holds Ph.D from Princeton University and is a former Professor and Director of GIDR. Currently, she is an Honorary Professor at the Institute.**

Her research interests include historical demography as well as field-based studies on problems of health, family planning, education and demographic transition. Her articles have appeared in several repuled journals. She has been a co-author of a book *Contraceptive Use and Fertility in India: A Case Study of Gujarat* (Sage Publications, New Delhi, 1995), and of *India in the 21st Century* along with Tim Dyson and Robert Cassen, both of London School of Economics (Oxford University Press, 2004). She has co-edited (with John Simons and Peter Berman), *Maternal Education and Child Survival: Pathways and Evidence* (Vikas Publishing House, Delhi, 1997); *Abortion in India: Ground Reality* (jointly with Vimala Ramachandran), New Delhi, Routledge, 2007; and *Midwifery & Maternal Health in India: Situation Analysis & Lessons from the Field*, CMHS Monograph No. 1, Indian Institute of Management, Ahmedabad, 2010.

During 1994-2008, she served as a co-ordinator of a network of non-governmental organisations (NGOs) and researchers, known as Health-Watch, which engaged in dialogue with policy makers, donors, researchers and activists on various gender-sensitive population and health policy issues. Beginning March 2008, she was awarded National Professorship for two years by Indian Council for Social Science Research, which is a parent body of all social science research institutes in India. Having been elected as the President of Asian Population Association for 2009-10, she organised the first international conference of the Association in New Delhi during November 2010.

Recent Publications

Abortion in India: Ground Reality (edited jointly with Vimala Ramachandran), New Delhi, Routledge, 2007.

Improving the Child Sex Ratio: Role of Policy and Advocacy, in *Economic and Political Weekly*, Vol 43, Nos. 12 and 13, March 22-April 4, 2008, pp 34-37.

"Assessment of the Impact of SEWA's Maternal Health Interventions, Maternal Health Project Paper 1, Gujarat Institute of Development Research, May 2008.

"Access to Drugs in Public Health Facilities in Tamil Nadu", Maternal Health Project Paper 2, Gujarat Institute of Development Research, June 2008.

"Same Policy Goals but Divergent Strategies: India's National Population Policy vs. State-specific Policies", in: Wong Siu-lun and Wang Cangbai (eds.), *Population Policies and Development in China and India: Comparative Perspective*, Centre of Asian Studies, The university of Hong Kong, 2009, pp. 139-161.

"Demographic Transition in India", in: Yogesh Atal (ed.), *Sociology and Social Anthropology in India*, ICSSR survey of Advances in Research, Pearson, New Delhi, 2009, pp. 359-391.*Midwifery & Maternal Health in India: Situation Analysis & Lessons from the Field* (ed.), CMHS Monograph No. 1, Indian Institute of Management, Ahmedabad, 2010.

1

Sanitation in India with Focus on Toilets and Disposal of Human Excreta

What is sanitation?

Sanitation refers to safe handling of many types of waste products. By safe handling we mean ensuring safety in collection, storage, treatment and disposal and if possible, reuse after treatment of all types of waste products. We generate a lot of waste in the form of human excreta (feaces and urine), solid kitchen wastes, household wastewater and storm water, sewage effluents, industrial waste products, hazardous wastes (including those from hospitals and chemical/radioactive and other dangerous substances) from industrial units or power plants. A large number of organisations and individuals have been engaged world over in innovative research and management of waste products and also in devising safe ways or processes in treatment or disposal or storage of wastes so that the environment is not damaged and polluted and any kind of life on our planet is not threatened.

India may claim that its ancient civilisation gave a lot of importance to sanitation by developing and constructing water storage facilities and drainage systems. However, in the 20th century India very little evidence of that is known to exist except in small pockets. The general lack of concern for basic hygiene and sanitation evident both in rural and urban areas was in fact articulated by Gandhiji, who famously remarked that, *"a sense of national or social sanitation is not a virtue among us. We may take a kind of a bath, but we do not mind dirtying the well or the tank or the river by whose side or in which we perform ablution"*. He was equally distressed by the fact that members of a certain community, labelled as 'untouchables' were required to perform the task of carrying and disposing of the 'night soil'.

The management and disposal of any kind of waste including the sewage effluents and industrial waste products in water sources and thereby contaminating them need serious discussion and interventions. However, this paper dwells on only one factor in some depth, i.e., the availability of toilets and the disposal of human excreta by building toilets in the context of equity. I first discuss the availability of toilet facility at the household level in India by examining the available information on households having toilets over time and variations across regions. The next section deals with the health impact of improper disposal of or handling of human excreta, especially that of young children. Next, I examine the sociological, cultural and economic factors hindering the use of toilets and the consequences of open defecation especially on women. The role of caste and efforts to restore human dignity among and rights of the scavenging community is discussed next along with a brief discussion on the design of individual toilets and community complexes such that the need to handle excreta by humans is eliminated. Lastly, some questions are raised for further reflection and research.

Data Sources

In India, data on toilet facility including on the type of toilet facility (such as flush system, septic tank, service type) have been available from several sources from 1981 onwards. They are generally tabulated for rural and urban areas at state level. The major sources of such data are the decennial Indian Census from 1981 onwards, the periodic surveys on housing conditions conducted by the National Sample Survey Organisation (NSSO), the three National Family Health Surveys (NFHS) conducted in 1992-93, 1998-99 and 2005-06 and the data collected by the Ministry of Drinking Water and Sanitation under the Total Sanitation Campaign (TSC).

In 1981 and 1991, the Indian Census asked only a simple question in the household schedule whether the household had any toilet facility. The information was tabulated separately for rural and urban areas for all the states. In the 2001 census, all households were asked to indicate the type of toilet they had, if they had a toilet. The toilets were classified as: water closet, pit latrine or any other type. The 2011

Census collected detailed information within broad types and asked households whether their flush latrines were connected to piped sewer system, or to a septic tank or had some other system for disposal. The pit latrine could be of two types – with slab and ventilated or without slab and therefore open to sky. If the households did not have any of the two types of toilets, information was collected on the way the night soil was disposed of – into open drain, serviced by humans or serviced by animals.

All the three NFHS surveys collected information on the type of toilet facilities available at the household level (flush or pit or none) and in 2005-06 in addition to these two types, information was sought on whether the household shared a toilet with other households. The last survey also collected information on how the children's stools were disposed of, which was tabulated by state, social groups, wealth index groups, and by the level of mother's education.

The NSS also collects information about the type of toilet facility (flush, septic tank, service latrine) and publishes it separately for rural and urban areas for the major states. These three sources of data are typically collected by asking questions to the head or some member of the household about various amenities they have including the type of toilet. In this paper, I have not analysed the data from various rounds of NSS in this paper.[1]

On the other hand, the data compiled by the Ministry of Drinking Water and Sanitation are based on the number of rural households that are provided subsidy to construct individual household latrines (IHHL) under the Total Sanitation Campaign (TSC). The scheme was launched first in 1986 under the Central

---

[1] The NSS data on access to toilet are somewhat higher than reported by the Census. The Census estimates are based on information collected from the entire population and not from a random sample of households as is the case with NSS. According to the 69th round of the NSS conducted in 2012-13, the percentage of rural households with toilets was 41, whereas according to 2011 Census, 31 per cent of rural households had toilets.

Rural Sanitation Programme primarily with the objective of improving the quality of life of the rural people and also to provide privacy and dignity to women (Government of India, [MODWS], 2010). However, systematic data on the number of household provided toilets with government support and those building with their own resources began to be collected only beginning 1999.[2,3] The annual estimates of number of households having constructed the toilets are converted into number of users of toilets on the assumption that one toilet would serve 10 persons.[3]

Access to toilets: Magnitude of the problem

Except for the estimates generated by the Ministry of Drinking Water and Sanitation under its programme, other sources by and large show similar level trend in the per centage of households having toilet facility. The data on per centage of households having some type of toilet facility from the four Indian Censuses are shown in Figure 1 for rural and urban areas separately and for the country as a whole. At all India level, availability of toilet increased from 14 per cent households having toilet in 1981 to 48 per cent in 2011; in other words, more than half of the Indian population or 650 million (or 130 million households) did not have any toilet facility in 2011.[4]

---

[2] The earlier rural sanitation programme called Total Sanitation Campaign has been revamped now into *Nirmal Bharat Abhiyan* in 2012 which aims to transform rural India into a *Nirmal Bharat* by adopting people centered and community led strategies with emphasis on awareness creation and demand generation for sanitary facilities in houses, schools and for cleaner environment. However, the only factor under the programme that is tracked is the number of toilets constructed.

[3] The Total Sanitation scheme was renamed as '*Nirmal Bharat Abhiyan*' in 2004, wherein the implementation is taken up with the Panchayat as a base unit. In 2003, the Government of India instituted Nirmal Gram Puraskar (NGP) for recognising, encouraging and facilitating the Panchayati Raj Institutions to promote and achieve total sanitation. The award is given to a village that becomes free of open defecation.

[4] Of the 1.1 billion people worldwide who are estimated to defecate in the open by the UN agencies, nearly 60 per cent live in India.

Figure 1: Percentage of Households Having Toilet Facility, by Place of Residence, India, 1981-2011

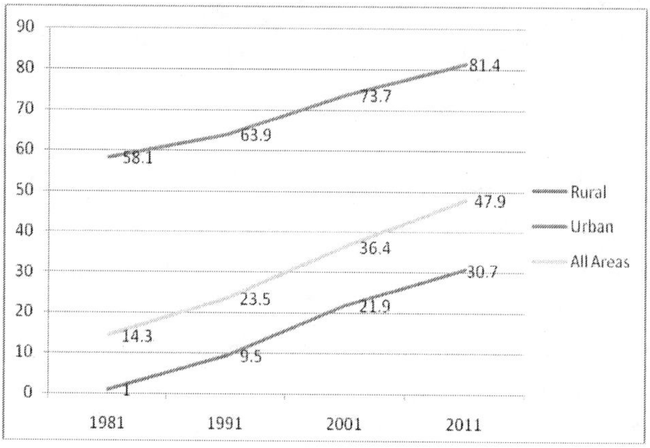

There have, however, been vast differences between rural areas and urban areas in the availability of toilet facilities. From barely 1 per cent of rural households having a toilet in 1981, almost 31 per cent reported having a toilet in 2011. In other words only three out of 10 rural households even today have their own toilet.[5] The situation in urban India has been significantly better; from 58 per cent urbanites having toilet facility in 1981, the percentage increased to 81 in 2011. Yet, even in cities and towns, one in five households has no toilet and members use open spaces (especially children) near their residence, public toilets, and railway tracts to defecate.

It may be noted that the estimates of the percentage of households and individuals having access to toilets according to *Nirmal Bharat Abhiyan* (NBA) for the Census year 2011, far exceed those available from the Census not only for India but for all the states. According to NBA, by

[5] When the 2011 Census data on household amenities were released, what made news and drew national and international attention was that 63 per cent of households reported to own telephone or mobile but only 48 per cent reported having toilet facility. In rural areas 54 per cent have phones but only 31 per cent have toilet facility.

2011, 68 per cent of population was covered by sanitation as against 32 per cent reported by the 2011 Census. Clearly, the methodology of estimating the users of toilets on the basis of funds disbursed for constructing them is problematic.[6]

Type of Toilet Facilities

In India, along with the overall decrease in the proportion of households without any kind of toilet facility, that of the users of pit toilet has also decreased. Instead, the use of flush toilet, requiring at least ten litres of water per flush, has increased over time, both in rural and urban areas according to the NFHS data as shown in Figure 2. In the country as a whole (rural and urban together), the percentage of households using flush toilets increased from 21 to 29 per cent between 1992-93 and 2005-06. According to the Census, the availability of flush toilet doubled from 18 to 36 per cent in the country between 2001 and 2011 and that of the pit latrine and other types decreased from 18 to 10 per cent. The remaining 54 to 56 per cent of households have no toilets and use whatever open space available near or away from their place of residence.

Figure 2: Type of Toilet Facilities in India According to NFHS, 1992-06

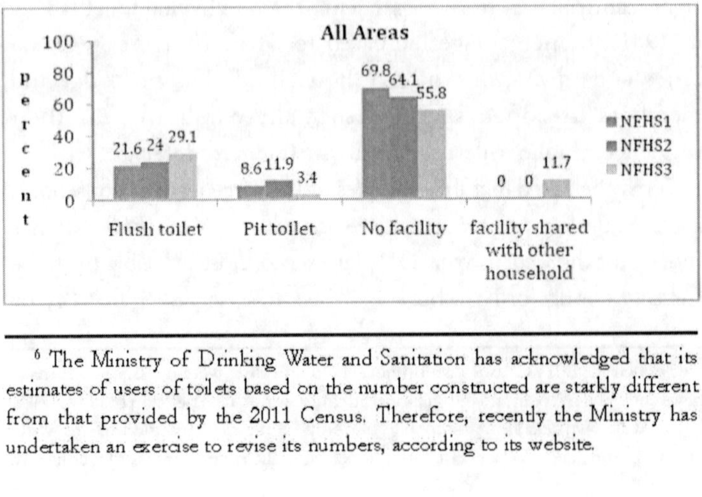

[6] The Ministry of Drinking Water and Sanitation has acknowledged that its estimates of users of toilets based on the number constructed are starkly different from that provided by the 2011 Census. Therefore, recently the Ministry has undertaken an exercise to revise its numbers, according to its website.

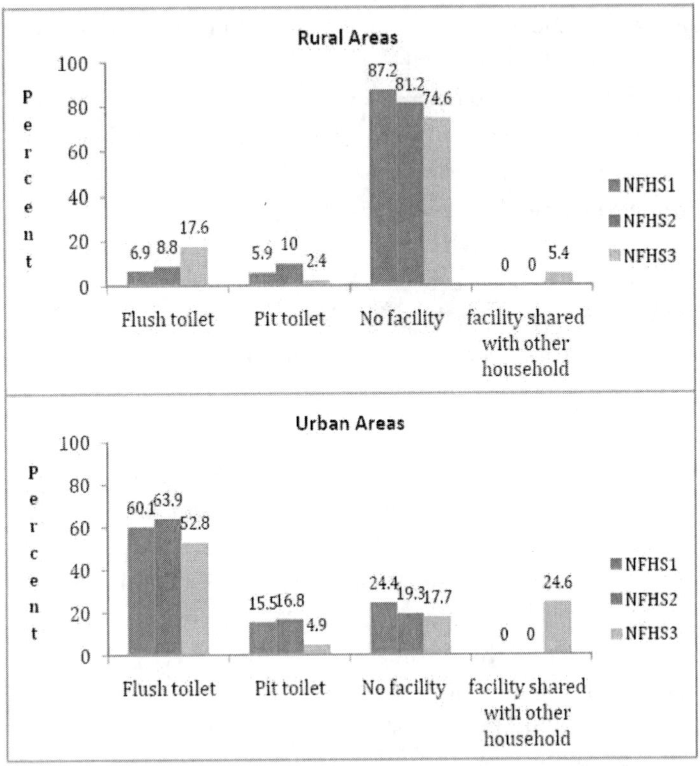

The 2005-06 NFHS survey, taking note of the urban reality of housing conditions, made a distinction between households having their own independent toilet and those who shared toilets with other households and noted that nearly a quarter of the urban households in India shared a toilet with other households, which are typically connected to sewer system; they may or may not have built in flush system.

The popularity of flush toilets both in rural and urban areas needs some serious thought and action. A typical flush toilet operates with a minimum of about 10 litres of water per flush and well-functioning sewer or drainage system. Given the water scarcity in India in most places and poorly maintained or non-existent sewer system in urban areas and practically non-existent sewer system in rural areas, the flush toilets are not the solution for majority of the areas. As Narain argues, water is a precious community or resource and cannot be used to transport human excreta (Narain, 2002). At individual or household level, having a flush toilet may be desirable, even though it uses good quality water. But the implications of it in terms of clogged sewers, how they are cleaned and who cleans them are serious issues that need serious attention before advocating flush toilets. Using appropriate technology, the toilets designed by Sulabh International and similar experiments by others appears to offer viable solution to make the country open defecation free.[7]

State Disparities in Availability of Toilet Facilities

As is true with respect to any development indicator, the situation with regard to availability of toilets is quite poor in the backward states like Bihar, Madhya Pradesh and Odisha. Figures 3.1(a) to 3.1(c), based on the 2001 and 2011 Census data presented for select states show some improvement over the decade; however it is disturbing to note that the improvement between 2001 and 2011 in the poor performing states was much less than in those states that were relatively much better in the initial period. Thus, for example, both Kerala and Punjab have reported significant increase in the households having toilet between 2001 and 2011. In Kerala, the percentage of households having own toilet increased from 77 in 2001 to 95 in 2011; implying that only five per cent of the households were without toilet facilities (seven per cent in rural and three per cent in urban areas) in 2011. In

[7] Sulabh's low-cost, pour flush toilet, made with locally available material needs only about 1.5 to 2 litres of water, saves precious water and is affordable for most people, especially in rural areas. It is connected to two pits, which are used alternatively to ensure that the system stays in operation.

Punjab also the increase in the per centage of households with toilets was equally impressive; from 45 per cent in 2001 to almost 80 per cent in 2011. This was true both in rural and urban areas. The per centage of households without toilet decreased from 67 to 30 per cent in rural areas and from 33 to less than 8 per cent in urban areas.

At the other end of the spectrum, Odisha recorded only a marginal improvement in provision of toilet facilities between 2001 and 2011 – from six to 13 per cent in rural areas and from 53 to 63 per cent in urban areas. Unfortunately, the disparities and gap between relatively progressive states and those that lag behind are increasing in access to toilets as on many other development indicators. Data on the availability of toilet in all the states of India for 2001 and 2011 are shown in Annex Table. Interestingly, the situation with respect to the availability of toilets is significantly better in smaller states than in large states.

Figure 3(a): Percentage of Households without Latrine and With Open Drain Facility-All India and Select States, 2001-11 All Areas

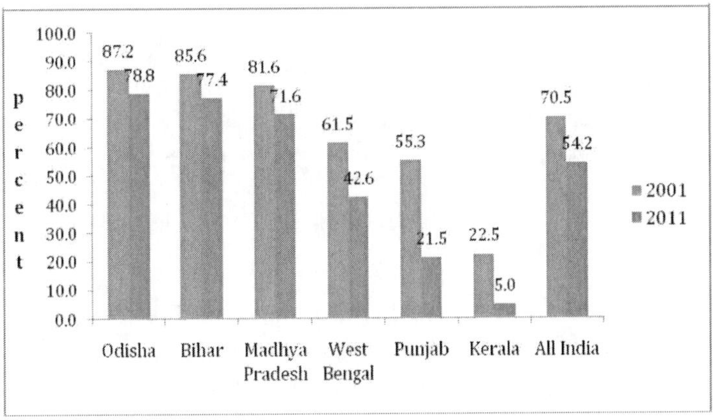

Figure 3(b): Percentage of Households Without Latrine and With Open Drain Facility-Rural Areas

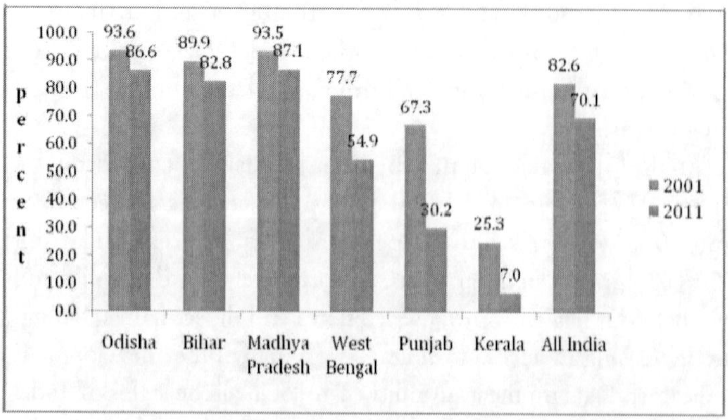

Figure 3(c): Percentage of Households Without Latrine and With Open Drain Facility-urban Areas

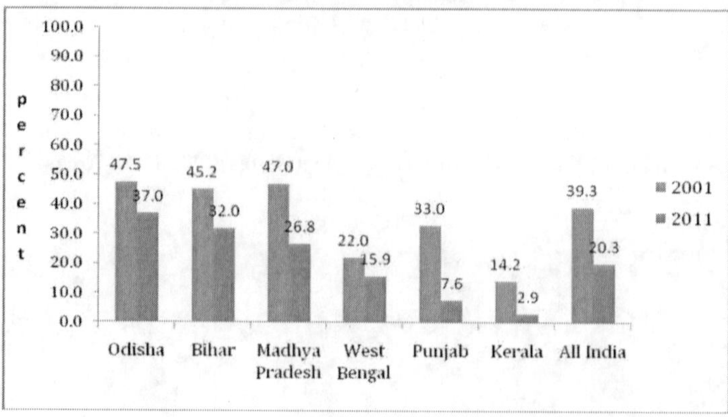

Another factor to be noted is that under the Total Sanitation Campaign, India may have built millions of toilets but according to one estimate 20 per cent of them are defunct. They are used as store rooms or to keep cattle. Among the states, where the percentage of such defunct toilets is staggeringly high are Jharkhand, Chattisgarh, Bihar and Uttar Pradesh with between 67 to 32 per cent defunct toilets ((Down to Earth, 2014). The cost to the national exchequer is huge, since the government has been giving subsidy to many of the households to build toilets.

Disposal of Children's Stools

Proper disposal of children's stools is very important in preventing spread of diaarhoea and other related diseases. Children's stools are considered harmless although from the point of health consequences they are loaded with harmful germs. The third NFHS survey of 2005-06 had collected information on how the families dispose of stool of children under five years of age. The findings were quite shocking and showed that stools of 79 per cent of children was disposed of unsafely; meaning it was thrown in garbage, left open unattended or rinsed into a drain or a ditch. Overall, less than 12 per cent of children used a toilet; the per centage of children using toilets was six in rural areas and 27 in urban areas. The stool of a little over nine per cent was disposed of into toilet or buried; implying safe disposal. Even in the households that had improved toilet facilities within their homes, only 30 per cent of the children used the toilet. Apparently, both the mothers and children fear the use of toilets by even four and five years old and are therefore not trained or encouraged to use.

As shown in Figures 4 and 5, inverse correlation is observed between the percentage of children, whose stool is disposed of unsafely and wealth index and maternal education.? Conversely, with the increase in wealth and level of mother's education, the percentage of households disposing children's stool safely increases. However, the fact that 35 to 39 per cent of those households falling in the highest quintile on wealth index or those with mothers' education of 12 or more years, do not dispose of children's stool safely is quite disturbing. Clearly, either the absence of the knowledge or the practice of basic hygiene in spite of presumably having the knowledge of association between exposed stool and health hazards, calls for serious overhaul in our education as well as civic sense. Among the SC or ST or backward caste households, between eight and nine out of 10 households did not dispose of children's stool safely as shown in Figure 6.

Figure 4: Percentage of Children Whose Stool Disposed of Unsafely by Wealth Index, 2005-06

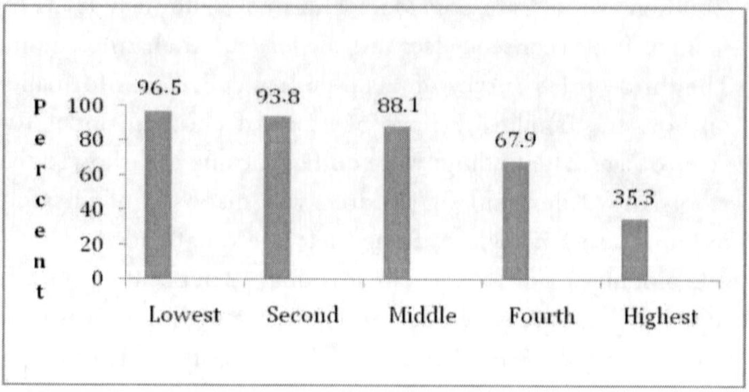

Figure 5: Percentage of Children Whose Stool Disposed of Unsafely by Education Level, 2005-06

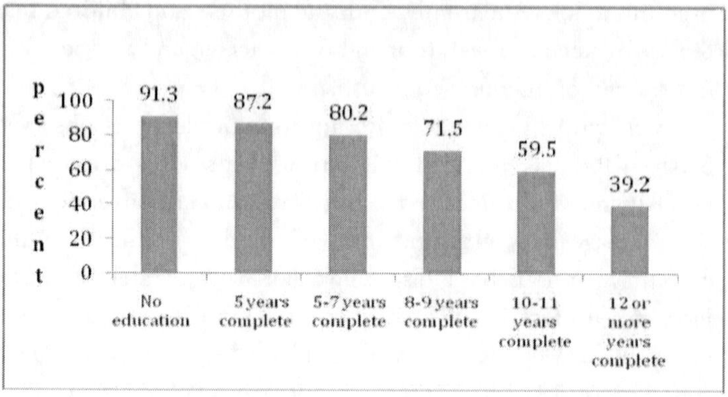

Figure 6: Percentage of Children Whose Stool Disposed of Unsafely by Caste NFHS, 2005-06

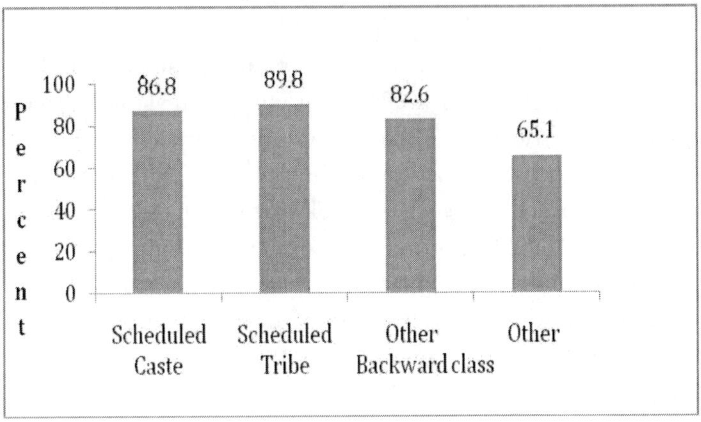

Note: Safe disposal means child is using toilet or if not using toilet, the stool is either rinsed into toilet or is buried.

There were state-specific differences in the manner in which children's stool was disposed. Among the larger states, Kerala was at one end of the spectrum, where 74 per cent of households reported safe disposal, and Odisha was at the other end where only seven per cent of households reported safe disposal. The other states where very low percentage of respondents reporting safe disposal were Rajasthan and Madhya Pradesh; only 10-11 per cent reported safe disposal. Overall development of state is important to explain state level differences, but the hold of tradition and beliefs are important in understanding whether and how children's stools are handled. In spite of some improvement evident in recent years, India is not likely to achieve the millennium development goal of reducing by half, the proportion of people without sustainable access to safe drinking water and sanitation by 2015.

Health Impact

Improved sanitation can have significant positive impact on health of household members and particularly on that of children. The provision and consistent use of sanitation isolates contaminated faeces from the environment breaking down the faecal-oral transmission of diseases. Human excreta are responsible for transmission of diarrhoea and soil-transmitted helminth infections (such as hookworm, roundworm) among children. In fact, faecal-oral diseases, dearrhoea being the most prevalent, represent the largest health burden associated with a lack of improved sanitation. Also, other infectious diseases including cholera, typhoid, infectious hepatitis, polio, cryptosporidiosis, and ascariasis are transmitted by improper disposal of excreta. Some studies have found that use of toilets potentially reduces diarrhoeal disease by an average of 36 per cent. (See: Esrey, 1991; Fewtrell, 2005).

An important correlation has been found between poor sanitation and children's development. Extensive research undertaken by Dean Spears (2012, 2013) in India and some African countries has shown that poor sanitation is responsible for the stunting of children under the age of five. Open defecation, which is widespread in India, can account for much or all of the excess stunting in India according to Spears.[8] Medical research has documented that environmental exposure to faecal germs could be an important cause of stunting. Stunting signifies children's failure to reach their developmental and cognitive capacities. It has been shown

---

8 The germs contained in faeces, when released into the environment, make their way onto children's fingers and feet, into their food and water. Flies are found in abundance in such area and also transmit germs. Exposure to these germs gives children diarrhoea, thereby compromising their nutritional status. Also, over the long term, the germs can cause changes in the tissues of children's intestines that prevent the absorption and use of nutrients in food, even when they do not seem sick.

that faecally-transmitted infections cause under-nutrition among children, which disappears with improved hygienic practices (Chambers, 2011).

Another important observation has been where population is denser, children would be more exposed to faecal pathogens. In other words, open defecation interacts with population density. Even those having toilet within their premises but live close to those who do not have and where children defecate in the neighbourhood are exposed to health hazards or contamination.

The general lack of awareness of personal hygiene, especially hand washing and the link between exposed faeces and transmission of germs, increases chances of infection among young children, because they are fed using fingers by their mothers. However, it has been difficult to change handwashing behaviour, because the people cannot see the connection between spread of contamination from the toilet or open defecation to food through hands.

Economic Argument

The health impact of inadequate sanitation leads to number of financial and economic costs including direct medical costs associated with treating sanitation-related illnesses. Poor sanitation leads to loss of productivity due to morbidity suffered from water-borne diseases. It increases the government costs of providing health services. Sanitation leads to time and effort losses due to distant or inadequate sanitation facilities, lower product quality resulting from poor water quality, reduced income from tourism (due to high risk of contamination and disease) and cleanup costs. Decrease in female literacy (due to low school attendance, where proper sanitation facilities do not exist) contributes to low economic growth.

According to the World Bank's Global Economics of Sanitation Initiative (ESI), inadequate sanitation imposes substantial economic losses. World Bank's Water and Sanitation Programme (WSP) anlaysed the available information on health burden (deaths and diseases) due to unsafe management of human excreta, domestic water-related time and other costs involved in fetching water from a distance, losses of tourism revenue, to measure the economic losses in India due to inadequate sanitation in year 2006. The study estimated that the total economic impact of inadequate sanitation in India amounted to Rs 2.44 trillion in a year. This was equivalent of 6.4 per cent of India's GDP in 2006 and per person annual impact or Rs 2,180 (World Bank, 2006). The country can neither afford nor accept such costs that far exceed the investments in sanitation.

Sociological Issues

Notions of purity and attitude towards excreta matters are complex among Indians. The urine and excreta of cows are considered sacred and so handled without any compunction. Among 62 per cent of rural households, the floor is plastered with mud – which is typically cowdung mixed with mud, water and straws and spread typically by women exposed to the harmful bacteria found in the cowdung. Cattle excreta have E coli that can be passed in the manure (faeces) of young calves and other cattle. Animals do not have to be unwell to transmit *E. coli* to humans. Symptoms of *E. coli* include watery or bloody diarrhoea, fever, abdominal cramps, nausea, and vomiting. Young children playing on such floors are more likely to contract infection and develop severe symptoms. Mothers handling cowdung, if do not wash hands thoroughly can infect children while feeding, cooking or handling water. Similarly, children's excreta are considered harmless although from the point of health consequences, it is loaded with harmful germs.

Open defecation is the societal norm in many communities and is often argued that people prefer open fields and feel claustrophobic in an enclosed area so that even when toilets are constructed, at least men prefer to go out to the field. However, women are affected to a great extent by the lack of toilets within the household. Both in rural areas and urban areas, women have to go in groups at twilight hours to defecate. Women defecating in the open are not only exposed to the risk of hygiene, but they face threats of harassment, teasing, lewd remarks and even rape in open fields after dark. The recent case of raping and killing two girls in Uttar Pradesh who had left home in to relieve themselves is a telling example of the vulnerability of women and lack of safety they face. At the community level, it raises the issue of neglected problem of safe sanitation.

Women may be responsible for fetching water, household cleanliness, but their own hygiene and sanitation needs receive scant attention from the men of the households. The initiatives such as Community Led Total Sanitation (CLTS) have tried to develop local solutions to build and provide low-cost latrines, built with local materials. By focussing on local mobilisation, it aims to bring about behavioural change. However, it is amply evident that infrastructure neither guarantees access nor equity. The sanitation needs of women differ from that of men but the policy of providing toilets with subsidy obviate such differences. There are even reports that the subsidy provided by the government is used for building compound, adding a room rather than building a toilet obviating the dire need of women in the household.

Also, girls are denied often their right to education, because their schools lack from private and decent sanitation facilities. Despite government efforts to improve the sanitation in schools, the 2013 Pratham report has shown that 26 per cent of rural schools do not have drinking water available for children, 37 per cent of the schools do not have useable toilets and more than 46 per cent or nearly half the schools do not have usable toilets for girls (Pratham, 2014). During menstruation, girls remain absent from going to school because it is an embarrassment to come to school, when there are no separate toilet facilities for them. In fact, some reports, claim almost quarter of girls drop out of school when they reach puberty.

Hold of Caste Hierarchy

In India, the task of cleaning sewers in urban areas or emptying pit latrines (of those who have) is done by members of certain community. They are sanitary workers or underground drainage cleaners and are engaged in unprotected, high risk jobs, and suffer from dangers of working in conditions that are even life-threatening. The manual scavengers are treated as untouchable – they are outside the caste structure –and face complete social exclusion. Manual scavenging as practiced in India is not only a water and sanitation issue but is a health and social issue with stigma, lack of dignity and discrimination as the core concern. The societal attitude towards manual scavengers remains a challenge in our country. It is also a gender issue since majority of scavengers is women, who face double burden of being women, belonging to the scavenger community.

An Act prohibiting manual scavenging was passed in 1993. However, it was enacted from the sanitation perspective and the Ministry of Housing and Poverty Alleviation that was supervising but did not fix the state's liability. So, many states did not even formulate statuettes under the Act, claiming they're free from manual scavenging. The new Bill passed in September 2013 looks at manual scavenging from the point of restoring human dignity and human rights. It speaks about rehabilitation, drafted by the ministry of social justice and empowerment. The Bill has broadly defined manual scavengers and does not address to the concerns of underground drainage cleaners, which mostly work without safety gear or masks. The issue is very complex. We need to understand the hidden caste/religious construction of scavenging and the scavenger's identity. The question still remains in caste-ridden society with increased use of water-saving disposal technology, whether the need for manually removing excreta may become unnecessary, that eliminate scavenging as an occupation, but will remove scavengers thereby as a community?

Community Involvement

There have been a few notable successful efforts, mainly by Non-Governmental Organisations (NGOs) to construct and maintain toilets. Sulabh International, for example, has designed a low-cost water-seal toilets for individual household that do not require manual scavengers to service. It has also built pay-and-use toilet complexes in cities for those who cannot build toilets within their houses because of cost or space constraints. It has thus addressed the twin issues of provision of clean toilets and the rehabilitation of scavenger community by inculcating a sense of dignity, promoted first in Bihar, community complexes have been built in many Indian cities. According to Sulabh International, 1.2 million toilet units have been constructed and nearly 8,000 pay-and-use toilet blocks have been constructed in many urban areas that have become quite popular among migrant workers, temporary visitors and those who do not have space or access to own toilets.[9] Dr Bindeshwar Pathak and Sulabh International have received many accolades and prizes for developing safe and environment-friendly toilet that reduces the need for scavenging.[10]

Efforts at involving communities have been undertaken by other NGOs in Pune and Mumbai, where the NGOs in partnership with the municipal corporations have built and maintain community toilet

---

[9] Besides a large number of publications of Sulabh International, some scholarly articles have also been written by others. (Among others see: Jha, 2010, Wei, Pillai and Maleku, 2014).

[10] Sulabh International has been helping to break the never-ending family cycle of scavenging and providing alternative economic opportunities so that women no longer have to clean toilets for the rest of their lives and providing education to their children.

blocks fairly successfully. They have demonstrated that partnership between municipal corporations and communities can improve sanitary conditions for poor people (Burra, Patel and Kerr, 2003).

Under the total Sanitation Campaign, Haryana state shifted the implementation from a top-down construction-based approach to generating awareness about sanitation through involvement of NGOs and village communities through Panchayati Raj Institutions, women's groups and others. The focus has been on changing the behaviour by communicating about the disadvantages of open defecation. As a result, the state of Haryana has become defecation free.

On the other hand, an NGO in Tamil Nadu – Gramalaya – has been advocating different low-cost toilet models using local materials, which are affordable and acceptable to local communities. Popularly known as eco-san toilets, toilet blocks have been designed for schools, small children in Anganwadis.

Many of these involve local communities, take into account of their needs and have yielded positive results. There is a need to popularise the use of toilets ensuring with dignity. Evidently, the top-down, subsidy-based model neither has led to sustainability, nor behavioural change, nonetheless many questions remain.

What Needs to be Done, What Could be Done?

Instead of being prescriptive, I would like to raise a few questions for us to ponder on, because there are no simple answers and many dimensions ought to be taken into account before coming up with solutions to the problem of open defecation.

- From all accounts, the Total Sanitation Campaign has been far from perfect in its outcome and implementation. Many have alluded to the faulty design, methodology and approach, the question is: Even at this stage, what can be done differently to bring about some change in the behaviour of people?

- Why do many of the latrines built remain unused or become dysfunctional? Is it simply because of the poor material or unfinished installation? Or some other reasons, which remain unarticulated and unstated?
- What cultural norms surround the sanitation practices in India still hamper use of toilets? Will the recently much publicised rape instance would trigger the need for changing the mindset at all levels including the household decision makers?
- What kind of policies would stimulate behavioural change and bring about a reduction in open defecation?
- What are the supply-side problems in implementing sanitation programmes, and how can we minimise leakages and bureaucratic apathy?
- Is it possible to develop innovative technologies like "next generation toilet" that would kill pathogens, is self-contained, is affordable, and that people want to use?
- Would the campaign like 'no toilet, no bride' work to change the attitude?

These are a few questions the research community should focus on, collect scientific evidence and move forward if we want the country to remove the blot of being living in unhygienic environment. Gandhiji once said 'sanitation is more important than Independence'; because sanitation is linked to human health and dignity.

References

Burra, S.S. Patel and T. Kerr, 2003. "Community-designed, built and managed toilet blocks in Indian cities", *Environment and Urbanisation,* Vol. 15, No. 2, pp. 11-32.

Chambers, R. 2011. "The future of DIFD's programme in India", http://www.publications.parliament.uk/pa/cm201011/cmselect/cmintdev/writev/616/m16.htm accessed on 5th June 2014.

Down to Earth, 2014, "India's Sanitation Programme: Mission Possible", *Down to Earth,* January 16, 2014, pp. 30-37.

Esrey S.A., J.B. Potash, L. Roberts and C. Shiff C, 1991."Effects of Improved Water Supply and Sanitation on Ascariasis, Diarrhoea, Dracunculiasis, Hookworm Infection, Schistosomiasis and Trachoma"*Bulletin of the World Health Organisation* Vol. 69, No. 5, pp. 609-21.

Fewtrell, L, et. al., 2005."Water, Sanitation, and Hygiene Interventions to Reduce Diarrhoea in Less Developed Countries: A Systematic Review and Meta-Analysis" *Lancet Infectious Diseases* Vol. 5, No. 1, pp. 42-52.

Government of India, Ministry of Drinking Water and Sanitation (MoDWS), 2010. Guidelines: Central Rural Sanitation Programme, Total Sanitation Campaign, June 2010. New Delhi.

Jha, P.K. 2010."Health and social benefits from improving community hygiene and sanitation: an Indian experience", *International Journal of Environmental Health Research,* Vol. 13, September. pp. 133-140.

Kumar, A. and A. Taunk, 2010. "A study of sanitation of toilets in elementary and senior secondary schools located in rural areas of Uttarakhand state in India", *International Journal of Sociology and Anthropology,* Vol. 2, no. 8, pp. 178-84.

Narain, S. 2002. "The flush toilet is ecologically mindless", *Down To Earth,* Vol. 10, No. 19 February 28.

Pratham, 2013. *Annual Status of Education Report ASER 2013 Rural.*

Spears, D. 2012 "Effects of rural sanitation on infant mortality and human capital: Evidence from India's total sanitation campaign", https://www.dartmouth.edu/~neudc2012/docs/paper_86.pdf accessed on June 2, 2014.

Spears, D. 2013, "The nutritional value of toilets: How much international variation in child height can sanitation explain?"

http://riceinstitute.org/wordpress/wp-content/uploads/downloads/2013/07/Spears-height-and-sanitation-6-2013.pdf accessed on June 2, 2014.

World Bank, Water and Sanitation Programme (WSP), 2006. *The Economic Impact of Inadequate Sanitation in India,* New Delhi.

Wei, F., V. Pillai and A. Maleku, 2014. "Sanitation in India: Role of women's education", *Health Science Journal,* Vol. 8, No. 1, pp. 90-101.

Annexure 1: Percentage of Households Having Toilet Facility in India, by State and Place of Residence, 2001 and 2011

States	*Total*		*Rural*		*Urban*	
	2001	*2011*	*2001*	*2011*	*2001*	*2011*
India	*36.4*	*46.9*	*21.9*	*30.7*	*73.7*	*81.4*
Major States						
Andhra Pradesh	33.0	49.6	18.1	32.2	78.1	86.1
Assam	64.6	64.9	59.6	59.6	94.6	93.7
Bihar	19.2	23.1	13.9	17.6	69.7	69.0
Chhatisgarh	14.2	24.6	5.2	14.5	52.6	60.2
Gujarat	44.6	57.3	21.7	33.0	80.5	87.7
Haryana	44.5	68.6	28.7	56.1	80.7	89.9
Himachal Pradesh	33.4	69.1	27.7	66.6	77.2	89.1
Jammu & Kashmir	53.1	51.2	41.8	38.6	86.9	87.5
Jharkhand	19.7	22.0	6.6	7.6	66.7	67.2
Karnataka	37.5	51.2	17.4	28.4	75.2	84.9
Kerala	84.0	95.2	81.3	93.2	92.0	97.4
Madhya Pradesh	24.0	28.8	8.9	13.1	67.7	74.2
Maharashtra	35.1	53.1	18.2	38.0	58.1	71.3
Odisha	14.9	22.0	7.7	14.1	59.7	64.8
Punjab	56.8	79.3	40.9	70.4	86.5	93.4
Rajasthan	29.0	35.0	14.6	19.6	76.1	82.0
Tamil Nadu	35.2	48.3	14.4	23.2	64.3	75.1
Uttar Pradesh	31.4	35.6	19.2	21.8	80.0	83.1
Uttarakhand	45.2	65.8	31.6	54.1	86.9	93.6
West Bengal	43.7	58.8	26.9	46.7	84.8	85.0
Small States						
Andaman & Nicobar Islands	53.3	70.1	42.3	60.2	76.5	87.1
Arunachal Pradesh	56.3	62.0	47.3	52.7	87.0	89.5
Chandigarh	78.9	87.6	68.5	88.0	80.1	87.6
Dadra & Nagar Haveli	32.6	54.7	17.3	26.5	77.2	81.3
Daman & Diu	43.9	78.2	32.0	51.4	65.4	85.4
Delhi	78.0	89.5	62.9	76.3	79.0	89.8
Goa	58.6	79.7	48.2	70.9	69.2	85.3
Lakshadweep	89.2	97.8	93.1	98.1	83.8	97.7
Manipur	82.0	89.3	77.5	86.0	95.3	95.8
Meghalaya	51.2	62.9	40.1	53.9	91.6	95.7
Mizoram	89.0	91.9	79.7	84.6	98.0	98.5
Nagaland	70.6	76.5	64.6	69.2	94.1	94.6
Puducherry	49.9	68.4	21.4	39.0	65.0	82.0
Sikkim	63.4	87.2	59.4	84.1	91.8	95.2
Tripura	81.4	86.0	77.9	81.5	97.0	97.9

[**Source**: Registrar General of India, *Census of India 2011, Houses, Household Amenities and Assets*, Latrine facility.]

Annexure 2: Manner of Disposal of Child's Stools by Select Background Characteristics, NFHS-3, 2005-06

Background characteristics	*Manner of disposal of child's stools*								*Total*	*Percentage of Children whose stools are disposed of safely*
	Child used toilet	*Rinsed into toilet*	*Buried*	*Rinsed Into Drain Or ditch*	*Thrown into garbage*	*Left in the open*	*Other*	*Missing*		
Age										
<6	1.4	9.3	1.2	20.2	33.7	28.3	5.1	0.8	100.0	11.9
6-11	2.5	9.6	1.0	11.3	38.0	34.9	2.1	0.5	100.0	13.1
12-23	6.0	9.0	0.9	7.0	33.5	42.8	0.4	0.4	100.0	15.9
24-35	14.1	8.1	0.7	3.8	22.8	49.2	0.4	0.8	100.0	23.0
36-47	20.8	8.3	0.4	2.8	12.8	53.5	0.3	0.9	100.0	29.6
48-59	27.8	9.0	0.2	2.4	7.0	52.9	0.1	0.7	100.0	37.0
Place of Residence										
Urban	26.8	20.1	0.3	10.2	16.7	24.6	0.7	0.6	100.0	47.2
Rural	5.9	4.7	0.9	6.5	28.8	51.1	1.4	0.7	100.0	11.4
Level of Education										
No education	4.9	3.1	0.8	6.9	28.9	53.9	1.1	0.5	100.0	8.7
<5 years complete	7.0	5.1	0.8	8.4	26.0	49.9	2.3	0.6	100.0	12.8
5-7 years complete	10.9	8.2	0.7	8.9	26.5	42.6	1.5	0.8	100.0	19.8
8-9 years complete	15.4	12.1	1.0	8.1	25.5	35.7	1.3	0.9	100.0	28.5
10-11 years complete	22.7	17.3	0.6	7.3	19.3	31.2	0.9	0.7	100.0	40.5
12 or more Years complete	32.5	27.7	0.7	7.1	13.7	16.8	0.6	0.9	100.0	60.8
Religion										
Hindu	10.6	7.8	0.8	7.1	26.4	45.6	1.1	0.7	100.0	19.1
Muslim	13.8	11.0	0.6	9.5	24.7	38.4	1.6	0.4	100.0	25.4
Christian	18.3	17.7	1.3	8.6	13.9	38.4	1.2	0.6	100.0	37.4
Sikh	26.8	24.8	0.5	5.0	17.8	24.2	0.1	0.7	100.0	52.1
Buddhist /neoBudh	10.4	15.2	1.9	11.3	16.4	41.1	0.0	3.8	100.0	27.4
Jain	49.1	29.3	0.0	4.1	5.5	11.9	0.0	0.0	100.0	78.4
Other	4.2	3.5	3.1	6.4	12.9	66.9	2.1	0.8	100.0	10.8
Caste										
Scheduled Caste	7.0	5.5	0.7	8.2	29.0	47.7	1.3	0.7	100.0	13.2
Scheduled Tribe	4.1	4.7	1.4	6.2	21.2	60.1	1.7	0.6	100.0	10.2

Continues

Continued

Other Backward castes	9.2	7.4	0.8	6.8	27.3	47.0	0.7	0.8	100.0	17.4
Other	20.0	14.3	0.6	8.4	22.2	32.5	1.6	0.4	100.0	34.9
Don't know	11.1	5.8	2.3	6.6	16.3	51.1	6.0	0.9	100.0	19.2
Toilet shared										
Improved, not shared	30.4	23.4	0.5	7.1	15.7	21.1	1.1	0.7	100.0	54.2
Non improved or shared	5.3	4.0	0.9	7.6	28.8	51.6	1.2	0.6	100.0	10.2
Wealth Quintile										
Lowest	1.7	1.0	0.9	5.9	30.9	57.4	1.7	0.5	100.0	3.5
Second	3.0	2.4	0.8	7.8	30.3	53.3	1.6	0.8	100.0	6.2
Middle	6.2	4.7	1.0	7.5	28.9	50.0	1.0	0.7	100.0	11.9
Fourth	17.2	14.2	0.7	9.7	21.6	35.0	0.9	0.7	100.0	32.1
Highest	36.9	27.5	0.3	6.9	12.0	15.3	0.5	0.6	100.0	64.7
Total	**11.5**	**8.8**	**0.8**	**7.5**	**25.6**	**44.0**	**1.2**	**0.7**	**100.0**	**21.1**

***Note*:** Total includes mothers with missing information on education, religion, caste/tribe, and toilet facility, who are not shown separately.

Annexure 3: Disposal of Children's Stools by Major States, NFHS-3, 2005-06

State	*Manner of disposal of child's stools*								*Total*	*Percetage of Children whose stools are disposed of safely*
	Child used toilet	*Rinsed into toilet*	*Buried*	*Rinsed Into Drain Or ditch*	*Thrown into garbage*	*Left in the open*	*Other*	*Missing*		
India	**11.5**	**8.8**	**0.8**	**7.5**	**25.6**	**44.0**	**1.2**	**0.7**	**100.0**	**21.1**
Andhra Pradesh	7.2	11.8	0.2	1.5	9.2	68.4	0.1	1.7	100.0	19.2
Assam	7.1	6.5	0.4	7.5	41.9	34.1	2.4	0.2	100.0	14.0
Bihar	4.7	1.9	0.4	8.2	32.3	50.9	0.7	1.0	100.0	6.9
Delhi	39.0	22.4	0.5	6.8	13.9	17.2	0.1	0.2	100.0	61.8
Goa	16.1	27.9	0.3	6.7	17.2	29.1	1.4	1.3	100.0	44.2
Gujarat	23.2	14.3	0.3	5.7	10.9	44.0	0.7	1.0	100.0	37.8
Haryana	20.0	15.8	0.0	5.8	18.9	39.3	0.0	0.2	100.0	35.8
Himachal Pradesh	20.2	11.7	0.4	9.1	10.7	43.5	2.3	2.1	100.0	32.3

Continues

Continued

Jammu and Kashmir	15.9	17.4	0.2	9.4	4.9	51.8	0.2	0.2	100.0	33.5
Karnataka	7.2	11.8	0.2	1.5	9.2	68.4	0.1	1.7	100.0	19.2
Kerala	7.0	11.3	2.3	8.4	15.2	51.2	2.4	2.2	100.0	20.6
Madhya Pradesh	6.6	3.4	0.4	6.0	21.0	62.6	0.0	0.0	100.0	10.4
Maharashtra	20.2	18.2	1.3	8.5	15.5	34.8	0.3	1.2	100.0	39.7
Orissa	4.8	0.8	1.4	1.3	32.3	53.7	5.0	0.6	100.0	7.0
Punjab	26.6	25.2	0.4	3.9	17.9	25.3	0.0	0.8	100.0	52.2
Rajasthan	6.0	4.6	0.5	5.7	27.9	55.2	0.0	0.2	100.0	11.1
Tamil Nadu	13.2	6.8	2.1	7.3	28.7	40.7	1.1	0.1	100.0	22.1
Uttar Pradesh	10.8	5.3	0.6	9.0	39.0	34.6	0.2	0.5	100.0	16.8
West Bengal	11.2	6.2	0.6	13.7	32.1	30.1	6.1	0.0	100.0	18.0

Note: Question was asked to mothers whether any child under the age of five is living with her.

2

Welcome Speech

at

1st National Distinguished Lecture Series on Sociology of Sanitation; Environmental Sanitation, Public Health and Social Deprivation

by

Dr Bindeshwar Pathak

under

Sulabh International Centre for Action Sociology in Collaboration with Sulabh International Social Service Organisation National Distinguished Lecture Series on Sociology of Sanitation

Hon'ble Prof Yogendra Singh, Professor Emeritus of Sociology Centre for the Study of School Systems, School of Social Sciences, Jawaharlal Nehru University, Hon'ble Prof. Leela Visaria, Eminent Sociologist and Former Director, Gujarat Institute of Development Research, Ahmedabad, Hon'ble members from print and electronic media, distinguished participants, ladies and gentlemen. It is my privilege and honour to welcome you all on the occasion of the first in the series of lectures on 'Sociology of Sanitation'.

I welcome Prof Yogendra Singh, a towering figure in the world of academia, an international social scientist and a pioneer sociologist, whose contributions have received universal acclaim. His presence as well as his illuminating address will be key to enriching the debate on 'Sociology of Sanitation'.

I welcome Prof Leela Visaria, a former Professor and Director of Gujarat Institute of Development Research, who is currently, an Honorary Professor at the Institute. Her research interests include historical demography as well as field-based studies on problems of health, family planning, education and demographic transition. Her articles have appeared in several national and International scholarly journals. She has been the author of many books and has been associated with the network of nongovernmental organisations (NGOs) and researchers, known as Health-Watch, which is engaged in dialogue with policy makers, donors, researchers and activists on various gender-sensitive and health related policy issues. She is an internationally acclaimed sociologist and a role model for researchers, activists and policy makers. It is our privilege to have her as the speaker to deliver the First National Lecture on 'Sociology of Sanitation'. I am sure, her lecture will set a high value and standard to the ongoing debate on 'Sociology of Sanitation' and will act as beacon for the future work on the same.

As there are eminent speakers to follow, I will just confine myself to a few suggestions on the subject of 'Sociology of Sanitation'.

In 1985, I proposed the concept of action sociology and suggested that sociologists should not only study, and teach about society, norms, social behaviour etc., but also intervene in the problems of society with a view to solving them as well. This approach of widening the concept of sociology and not limiting it to teaching only, proved highly beneficial and helped the society at large. This concept of action sociology, outlined by me, was also put into practice in the Sulabh Sanitation Movement.

To put it very succinctly, putting the concept of action sociology into practice, I not only invented the Sulabh two-pit pour-flush compost toilet which acted as a tool to eliminate the scourge of manual scavenging by the untouchables, but also took the consequent action of liberating and rehabilitating these untouchable manual scavengers and bringing them into the mainstream of society on a par with others. Thus, the concept of action sociology was not only limited to study and teaching it, but also helped in solving the problems of society.

Prof Marion Talbot wrote a paper in 1896, on 'Sociology and Sanitation'. After that not much headway was made on the subject.

In January 2013, under the aegis of Sulabh International Centre for Action Sociology, the first National Conference on 'Sociology of Sanitation', was held in New Delhi in which the galaxy of luminaries, academicians and sociologists actively participated. In the said National Conference, I propounded the theory of 'Sociology of Sanitation' defining it as follows:

"Sociology of sanitation is a scientific study to solve the problems of society in relation to sanitation, social deprivation, water, public health, hygiene, ecology, environment, poverty, gender equality, welfare of children and empowering people for sustainable development and attainment of philosophical and spiritual knowledge to lead a happy life and to make a difference in the lives of others."

Standing before you today, I would like to enumerate that the concept of 'Sociology of Sanitation' will deal with the environment at three levels. One, the physical environment, the second, social environment and thirdly, the inner environment.

Now coming to the first level, i.e., the physical environment, I would like to say that it involves and includes provision of safe water, safe and hygienic disposal of liquid and solid waste, and deals with pollution of rivers, erosion of soil, felling of trees, global warming, climate change, etc. Herein, I would like to add that social medicine and social engineering could be included in the broad concept of sociology of sanitation at this level.

Secondly, the social environment will deal at three levels; individual to individual, individual to group and group to group, towards making a harmonious and happy society to live in peaceful co-existence with all for a happier world. There should be no conflict on the basis of religion, culture, customs, rituals, moral values etc. Instead of pursuing one's belief and fighting one another, it is better to take ideas from all the thoughts, beliefs, religions and cultures and to assimilate them in order to bring the feeling of oneness in society and amongst people.

There are conflicts of opinion among different religions and at the same time, there are also differences of opinion in a particular religion itself. Like the Hindus, who have many beliefs and where each one says that it is superior to the other. Islam has oneness of religion, but they too have different beliefs as in case of the Shias and Sunnis who in many cases are in conflict with each other. Likewise in Christianity, there are varying beliefs and where the Catholics and Protestants have also been known to be in conflict.

I would like to give you a small example. Suppose I find a child crying on the road. Should I not first take him in my lap, comfort him, give him sweets or fruit to eat, console him and try to find his parents? Or should I leave the child crying and try to find out to which religion he belongs. In the former alternative, humanity and kindness will speak, and my action will bring a cordial atmosphere in society. But in the latter it will only create hatred and ill-feeling.

The third is the level of inner environment. In inner environment, a man should be positive in nature, spiritual, kind to others and helpful towards solving the problems of both the society and the individual. A person who is philosophical, endowed with wisdom and spirituality, will naturally love all people and creatures in this world, we see around. The Vedas say *"I am a man, you are a man, and so are all men"*. This philosophy rings the message that all human beings are equal. So people should have the inner environment and conscience to try to wipe out the tears of others and make them smile, irrespective of religion and culture. The inner environment of a person can be helpful towards solving the problems of physical and social environment.

Here I would like to give you another example of the widows of Vrindavan which enumerates the level of inner environment. The Supreme Court of India was in seisin of a matter relating to the pitiable and appalling conditions prevalent amongst the widows of Vrindavan. At the intervention of the Supreme Court of India through National Legal Services Authority (NALSA) Sulabh International Social Service Organisation took up in the matter and provided them all round relief including monthly stipend thereby ameliorating their lives and living conditions. We succeeded in wiping out the tears and as one of them said "after Sulabh's intervention, our desire to die has changed to yearning to live".

To reiterate, the philosophy of 'Sociology of Sanitation', I want to say is that we should teach not only about physical environment but also the social and inner environment in 'Sociology of Sanitation'

I would like to conclude by quoting from one of the most illuminating emails received from a scholar studying in the South Korean National University, Jiyeon Park. Park had come to do research in Sulabh alongwith the other researchers belonging to South Korean National University and on a return she sent us an email which I am quoting verbatim... *"Oh! by the way I'm a double major one in economy and one in virtual design here in Seoul National University recently, for a design project I made a speech regarding the Sulabh Toilet Museum and got a good remarks ...*

Good Design means where members of community "communicates" toward virtue and ideal society with all heart ... and as a real-life example, I adopted the idea of Sulabh because the sanitation programme (mechanism) the museum and design of toilets (form) and the virtue of double emancipation (economic, social) + love and peace (meaning) are all coherent with this concept of Good Design ..."

Once again, I welcome you all, and hope that you will find the lectures of the eminent personalities on the dais of considerable interest and immense value.

Once again thank you all for coming today.